God's Utility Function

Richard Dawkins

A Phoenix Paperback

First published in Great Britain by Weidenfeld & Nicolson in 1995 as
River Out of Eden (Science Masters series)

This abridged edition published in 1996 by Phoenix
a division of Orion Books Ltd
Orion House, 5 Upper St Martin's Lane, London WC2H 9EA

This abridged edition contains the Preface and Chapter 4.

ISBN 1 85799 595 3

Typeset by Deltatype Ltd, Ellesmere Port, Cheshire
Printed in Great Britain by Clays Ltd, St Ives plc

CONTENTS

Preface

Nature, it seems is the popular name
For milliards and milliards and milliards
Of particles playing their infinite game
Of billiards and billiards and billiards.
— Piet Hein

Piet Hein captures the classically pristine world of physics. But when the ricochets of atomic billiards chance to put together an object that has a certain, seemingly innocent property, something momentous happens in the universe. That property is an ability to self-replicate; that is, the object is able to use the surrounding materials to make exact copies of itself, including replicas of such minor flaws in copying as may occasionally arise. What will follow from this singular occurrence, anywhere in the universe, is Darwinian selection and hence the baroque extravaganza that, on this planet, we call life. Never were so many facts explained by so few assumptions. Not only does the Darwinian theory command superabundant power to explain. Its economy in doing so has a sinewy elegance, a poetic beauty that outclasses even the most haunting of the world's origin myths. One of my purposes in writing this book has been to accord due recognition to the inspirational quality of our modern understanding of Darwinian life. There is more poetry in Mitochondrial Eve than in her mythological namesake.

The feature of life that, in David Hume's words, most 'ravishes into admiration all men who have ever contemplated it' is the complex detail with which its mechanisms – the mechanisms that Charles Darwin called 'organs of extreme perfection and complication' – fulfill an apparent purpose. The other feature of earthly life that impresses us is its luxuriant diversity: as measured by estimates of species numbers, there are some tens of millions of different ways of making a living. Another of my purposes is to convince my readers that 'ways of making a living' is synonymous with 'ways of passing DNA-coded texts on to the future.' My 'river' is a river of DNA, flowing and branching through geological time, and the metaphor of steep banks confining each species' genetic games turns out to be a surprisingly powerful and helpful explanatory device.

In one way or another, all my books have been devoted to expounding and exploring the almost limitless power of the Darwinian principle – power unleashed whenever and wherever there is enough time for the consequences of primordial self-replication to unfold. *River Out of Eden*, from which this extract is taken, continues this mission and brings to an extraterrestrial climax the story of the repercussions that can ensue when the phenomenon of replicators is injected into the hitherto humble game of atomic billiards . . .

God's Utility Function

My clerical correspondent of the previous chapter found faith through a wasp. Charles Darwin lost his with the help of another: 'I cannot persuade myself,' Darwin wrote, 'that a beneficent and omnipotent God would have designedly created the Ichneumonidae with the express intention of their feeding within the living bodies of Caterpillars.' Actually Darwin's gradual loss of faith, which he downplayed for fear of upsetting his devout wife Emma, had more complex causes. His reference to the Ichneumonidae was aphoristic. The macabre habits to which he referred are shared by their cousins the digger wasps, whom we met in the previous chapter. A female digger wasp not only lays her egg in a caterpillar (or grasshopper or bee) so that her larva can feed on it but, according to Fabre and others, she carefully guides her sting into each ganglion of the prey's central nervous system, so as to paralyze it *but not kill it*. This way, the meat keeps fresh. It is not known whether the paralysis acts as a general anesthetic, or if it is like curare in just freezing the victim's ability to move. If the latter, the prey might be aware of being eaten alive from inside but unable to move a muscle to do anything about it. This sounds savagely cruel but, as we shall see, nature is not cruel, only pitilessly indifferent. This is one of the hardest lessons for humans to learn. We cannot admit that things might be neither good nor evil, neither cruel nor kind, but simply callous – indifferent to all suffering, lacking all purpose.

We humans have purpose on the brain. We find it hard to look at anything without wondering what it is 'for,' what the motive for it is, or the purpose behind it. When the obsession with purpose becomes pathological it is called paranoia – reading malevolent purpose into what is actually random bad luck. But this is just an exaggerated form of a nearly universal delusion. Show us almost any object or process, and it is hard for us to resist the 'Why' question – the 'What is it for?' question.

The desire to see purpose everywhere is a natural one in an animal that lives surrounded by machines, works of art, tools and other designed artifacts; an animal, moreover, whose waking thoughts are dominated by its own personal goals. A car, a tin opener, a screwdriver and a pitchfork all legitimately warrant the 'What is it for?' question. Our pagan forebears would have asked the same question about thunder, eclipses, rocks and streams. Today we pride ourselves on having shaken off such primitive animism. If a rock in a stream happens to serve as a convenient stepping-stone, we regard its usefulness as an accidental bonus, not a true purpose. But the old temptation comes back with a vengeance when tragedy strikes – indeed, the very word 'strikes' is an animistic echo: 'Why, oh why, did the cancer/earthquake/hurricane have to strike *my* child?' And the same temptation is often positively relished when the topic is the origin of all things or the fundamental laws of physics, culminating in the vacuous existential question 'Why is there something rather than nothing?'

I have lost count of the number of times a member of the audience has stood up after a public lecture I have given and said something like the following: 'You scientists are very good at answering 'How' questions. But you must admit you're powerless when it comes to 'Why' questions.' Prince Philip, Duke of Edinburgh, made this very point when he was in an audience at Windsor addressed by my colleague Dr. Peter Atkins. Behind the question there is always an unspoken but never justified implication that since science is unable to answer 'Why' questions, there must be some other discipline that *is* qualified to answer them. This implication is, of course, quite illogical.

I'm afraid that Dr. Atkins gave the Royal Why fairly short shrift. The mere face that it is possible to frame a question does not make it legitimate or sensible to do so. There are many things about which you can ask, 'What is its temperature?' or 'What color is it?' but you may not ask the temperature question or the color question of, say, jealousy or prayer. Similarly, you are right to ask the 'Why' question of a bicycle's mudguards or the Kariba Dam, but at the very least you have no right to *assume* that the 'Why' question deserves an answer when posed about a boulder, a misfortune, Mt. Everest or the universe. Questions can be simply inappropriate, however heartfelt their framing.

Somewhere between windscreen wipers and tin openers on the one hand and rocks and the universe on the other lie living creatures. Living bodies and their organs are objects that, unlike rocks, seem to have purpose written all over them. Notoriously, of course, the apparent purposefulness of living bodies has dominated the classic Argument from Design, invoked by theologians from Aquinas to William Paley to modern 'scientific' creationists.

The true process that has endowed wings and eyes,

beaks, nesting instincts and everything else about life with the strong illusion of purposeful design is now well understood. It is Darwinian natural selection. Our understanding of this has come astonishingly recently, in the last century and a half. Before Darwin, even educated people who had abandoned 'Why' questions for rocks, streams and eclipses still implicitly accepted the legitimacy of the 'Why' question where living creatures were concerned. Now only the scientifically illiterate do. But 'only' conceals the unpalatable truth that we are still talking about an absolute majority.

Actually, Darwinians do frame a kind of 'Why' question about living things, but they do so in a special, metaphorical sense. Why do birds sing, and what are wings for? Such questions would be accepted as a shorthand by modern Darwinians and would be given sensible answers in terms of the natural selection of bird ancestors. The illusion of purpose is so powerful that biologists themselves use the assumption of good design as a working tool. As we saw in the previous chapter, long before his epoch-making work on the bee dance Karl von Frisch discovered, in the teeth of strong orthodox opinion to the contrary, that some insects have true color vision. His clinching experiments were

stimulated by the simple observation that bee-pollinated

flowers go to great trouble to manufacture colored pigments. Why would they do this if bees were color-blind? The metaphor of purpose – more precisely, the assumption that Darwinian selection is involved – is here being used to make a strong inference about the world. It would have been quite wrong for von Frisch to have said, 'Flowers are colored, therefore bees must have color vision.' But it was right for him to say, as he did, 'Flowers are colored, therefore it is at least worth my while working hard at some new experiments to test the hypothesis that they have color vision.' What he found when he looked into the matter in detail was that bees have good color vision but the spectrum they see is shifted relative to ours. They can't see red light (they might give the name 'infra yellow' to what we call red). But they can see into the range of shorter wavelengths we call ultraviolet, and they see ultraviolet as a distinct color, sometimes called 'bee purple.'

When he realized that bees see in the ultraviolet part of the spectrum, von Frisch again did some reasoning using the metaphor of purpose. What, he asked himself, do bees use their ultraviolet sense for? His thoughts returned full circle – to flowers. Although we can't see ultraviolet light, we can make photographic film that is sensitive to it, and we can make filters that are transparent to ultraviolet light but cut out 'visible' light. Acting on his hunch, von Frisch took some ultraviolet photographs of flowers. To his delight, he saw patterns of spots and stripes that no human eye had ever seen before. Flowers that to us look white or yellow are in fact decorated with ultraviolet patterns, which often serve as runway markers to guide the bees to the nectaries. The assumption of apparent purpose had paid off once again: flowers, if they were well designed, would exploit the fact that bees can see ultraviolet wavelengths.

When he was an old man, von Frisch's most famous work – on the dance of the bees, which we discussed in the last chapter – was called into question by an American biologist named Adrian Wenner. Fortunately, von Frisch lived long enough to see his work vindicated by another American, James L. Gould, now at Princeton, in one of the most brilliantly conceived experiments of all biology. I'll briefly tell the story, because it is relevant to my point about the power of the 'as if designed' assumption.

Wenner and his colleagues did not deny that the dance happens. They did not even deny that it contains all the information von Frisch said it did. What they did deny is that other bees read the dance. Yes, Wenner said, it is true that the direction of the straight run of the waggle dance relative to the vertical is related to the direction of food relative to the sun. But no, other bees don't receive this information from the dance. Yes, it is true that the rates of various things in the dance can be read as information about the distance of food. But there is no good evidence that the other bees read the information. They could be ignoring it. Von Frisch's evidence, the skeptics said, was flawed, and when they repeated his experiments with proper 'controls' (that is, by taking care of alternative means by which bees might find food), the experiments no longer supported von Frisch's dance-language hypothesis.

This was where Jim Gould came into the story with his exquisitely ingenious experiments. Gould exploited a long-known fact about honeybees, which you will remember from the previous chapter. Although they usually dance in the dark, using the straight-up direction in the vertical plane as a coded token of the sun's direction in the horizontal plane, they will effortlessly switch to a possibly more ancestral way of doing things if you turn on a light inside the hive. They then forget all about gravity and use the lightbulb as their token sun, allowing it to determine the angle of the dance directly. Fortunately, no misunderstandings arise when the dancer switches her allegiance from gravity to the lightbulb. The other bees 'reading' the dance switch their allegiance in the same way, so the dance still carries the same meaning: the other bees still head off looking for food in the direction the dancer intended.

Now for Jim Gould's masterstroke. He painted a dancing bee's eyes over with black shellac, so that she couldn't see the lightbulb. She therefore danced using the normal gravity convention. But the other bees following her dance, not being blindfolded, could see the lightbulb. They interpreted the dance as if the gravity convention had been dropped and replaced the lightbulb 'sun' convention. The dance followers measured the angle of the dance relative to gravity. Gould was, in effect, forcing the dancing bee to lie about the direction of the food. Not just lie in a general sense, but lie in a particular direction that Gould could precisely manipulate. He did the experiment not with just one blindfolded bee, of course, but with a proper statistical sample of bees and variously manipulated angles. And it worked. Von Frisch's original dance-language hypothesis was triumphantly vindicated.

I didn't tell this story for fun. I wanted to make a point about the negative as well as the positive aspects of the assumption of good design. When I first read the skeptical papers of Wenner and his colleagues, I was openly derisive. And this was not a good thing to be, even though Wenner eventually turned out to be wrong. My derision was based entirely on the 'good design' assumption. Wenner was not, after all, denying that the dance happened, nor that it embodied all the information von Frisch had claimed about the distance and direction of food. Wenner simply denied that the other bees read the information. And this was too much for me and many other Darwinian biologists to stomach. The dance was so complicated, so richly contrived, so finely tuned to its apparent purpose of informing other bees of the distance and direction of food. This fine tuning could not have come about, in our view, other than by natural selection. In a way, we fell into the same trap as creationists do when they contemplate the wonders of life. The dance simply had to be doing something useful, and this presumably meant helping foragers to find food. Moreover, those very aspects of the dance that were so finely tuned – the relationship of its angle and speed to the direction and distance of food – had to be doing something useful too. Therefore, in our view, Wenner just had to be wrong. So confident was I that, even if I had been ingenious enough to think of Gould's blindfold experiment (which I certainly wasn't), I would not have bothered to do it.

Gould not only was ingenious enough to think of the experiment but he also bothered to do it, because he was not seduced by the good-design assumption. It is a fine tightrope we are walking, however, because I suspect that Gould – like von Frisch before him, in his color research – had enough of the good-design assumption in his head to believe that his remarkable experiment had a respectable chance of success and was therefore worth spending time and effort on.

I now want to introduce two technical terms, 'reverse engineering' and 'utility function.' In this section, I am influenced by Daniel Dennett's superb book *Darwin's Dangerous Idea*. Reverse engineering is a technique of reasoning that works like this. You are an engineer, confronted with an artifact you have found and don't understand. You make the working assumption that it was designed for some purpose. You dissect and analyze the object with a view to working out what problem it would be good at solving: 'If I had wanted to make a machine to do so-and-so, would I have made it like this? Or is the object better explained as a machine designed to do such-and-such?'

The slide rule, talisman until recently of the honorable profession of engineer, is in the electronic age as obsolete as any Bronze Age relic. An archaeologist of the future, finding a slide rule and wondering about it, might note that it is handy for drawing straight lines or for buttering bread. But to assume that either of these was its original purpose violates the economy assumption. A mere straight-edge or butter knife would not have needed a sliding member in the middle of the rule. Moreover, if you examine the spacing of the graticules you find precise logarithmic scales, too meticulously disposed to be accidental. It would dawn on the archaeologist that, in an age before electronic calculators, this pattern would constitute an ingenious trick for rapid multiplication and division. The mystery of the slide rule would be solved by reverse engineering, employing the assumption of intelligent and economical design.

'Utility function' is a technical term not of engineers but of economists. It means 'that which is maximized.' Economic planners and social engineers are rather like architects and real engineers in that they strive to maximize something. Utilitarians strive to maximize 'the greatest happiness for the greatest number' (a phrase that sounds more intelligent than it is, by the way). Under this umbrella, the utilitarian may give long-term stability more or less priority at the expense of short-term happiness, and utilitarians differ over whether they measure 'happiness' by monetary wealth, job satisfaction, cultural fulfilment or personal relationships. Others avowedly maximize their own happiness at the expense of the common welfare, and they may dignify their egoism by a philosophy that states that general happiness will be maximized if one takes care of oneself. By watching the behaviour of individuals throughout their lives, you should be able to reverse-engineer their utility functions. If you reverse-engineer the behaviour of a country's government, you may conclude that what is being maximized is employment and universal welfare. For another country, the utility function may turn out to be the continued power of the president, or the wealth of a particular ruling family, the size of the sultan's harem, the stability of the Middle East or maintaining the price of oil. The point is that more than one utility function can be imagined. It isn't always obvious what individuals, or firms, or governments are striving to maximize. But it is probably safe to assume that they are maximizing something. This is because *Homo sapiens* is a deeply purpose-ridden species. The principle holds good even if the utility function turns out to be a weighted sum or some other complicated function of many inputs.

Let us return to living bodies and try to extract their

utility function. There could be many but, revealingly, it will eventually turn out that they all reduce to one. A good way to dramatize our task is to imagine that living creatures were made by a Divine Engineer and try to work out, by reverse engineering, what the Engineer was trying to maximize: What was God's Utility Function?

Cheetahs give every indication of being superbly designed for something, and it should be easy enough to reverse-engineer them and work out their utility function. They appear to be well designed to kill antelopes. The teeth, claws, eyes, nose, leg muscles, backbone and brain of a cheetah are all precisely what we should expect if God's purpose in designing cheetahs was to maximize deaths among antelopes. Conversely, if we reverse-engineer an antelope we find equally impressive evidence of design for precisely the opposite end: the survival of antelopes and starvation among cheetahs. It is as though cheetahs had been designed by one deity and antelopes by a rival deity. Alternatively, if there is only one Creator who made the tiger and the lamb, the cheetah and the gazelle, what is He playing at? Is He a sadist who enjoys spectator blood sports? Is He trying to avoid overpopulation in the mammals of Africa? Is He maneuvering to maximize David Attenborough's television ratings? These are all intelligible utility functions that might have turned out to be true. In fact, of course, they are all completely wrong. We now understand the single Utility Function of life in great detail, and it is nothing like any of those.

Chapter 1 will have prepared the reader for the view that the true utility function of life, that which is being maximized in the natural world, is DNA survival. But DNA is not floating free; it is locked up in living bodies and it has to make the most of the levers of power at its disposal. DNA sequences that find themselves in cheetah bodies maximize their survival by causing those bodies to kill gazelles. Sequences that find themselves in gazelle bodies maximize their survival by promoting opposite ends. But it is DNA survival that is being maximized in both cases. In this chapter, I am going to do a reverse-engineering job on a number of practical examples and show how everything makes sense once you assume that DNA survival is what is being maximized.

The sex ratio – the proportion of males to females – in wild populations is usually 50:50. This seems to make no economic sense in those many species in which a minority of males has an unfair monopoly of the females: the harem system. In one well-studied population of elephant seals, 4 percent of the males accounted for 88 percent of all the copulations. Never mind that God's Utility Function in this case seems so unfair for the bachelor majority. What is worse, a cost-cutting, efficiency-minded deity would be bound to spot that the deprived 96 percent are consuming half the population's food resources (actually more than half, because adult male elephant seals are much bigger than females). The surplus bachelors do nothing except wait for an opportunity to displace one of the lucky 4 percent of harem masters. How can the existence of these unconscionable bachelor herds possibly be justified? Any utility function that paid even a little attention to the economic efficiency of the community would dispense with the bachelors. Instead, there would be just enough males born to fertilize the females. This apparent anomaly, again, is explained with elegant simplicity once you understand the true Darwinian Utility Function: maximizing DNA survival.

I'll go into the example of the sex ratio in a little detail, because its utility function lends itself subtly to an economic treatment. Charles Darwin confessed himself baffled: 'I formerly thought that when a tendency to produce the two sexes in equal numbers was advantageous to the species, it would follow from natural selection, but I now see that the whole problem is so intricate that it is safer to leave its solution for the future.' As so often, it was the great Sir Ronald Fisher who stood up in Darwin's future. Fisher reasoned as follows.

All individuals born have exactly one mother and one father. Therefore the total reproductive success, measured in distant descendants, of all males alive must equal that of all females alive. I don't mean of *each* male and female, because some individuals clearly, and importantly, have more success than others. I am talking about the totality of males compared with the totality of females. This total posterity must be divided up between the individual males and females – not divided equally, but divided. The reproductive cake that must be divided among all males is equal to the cake that must be divided among all females. Therefore if there are, say, more males than females in the population, the average slice of cake per male must be smaller than the average slice of cake per female. It follows that the average reproductive success (that is, the expected number of descendants) of a male compared with the average reproductive success of a female is solely determined by the male-female ratio. An average member of the minority sex has a greater reproductive success than an average member of the majority sex. Only if the sex ratio is even and there is no minority will the sexes enjoy equal reproductive success. This remarkably simple conclusion is a consequence of pure armchair logic. It doesn't depend on any empirical facts at all, except the fundamental fact that all children born have one father and one mother.

Sex is usually determined at conception, so we may assume that an individual has no power to determine his or her (for once the circumlocution is not ritual but necessary) sex. We shall assume, with Fisher, that a parent might have power to determine the sex of its offspring. By 'power', of course, we don't mean power consciously or deliberately wielded. But a mother might have a genetic predisposition to generate a vaginal chemistry slightly hostile to son-producing but not to daughter-producing sperms. Or a father might have a genetic tendency to manufacture more daughter-producing sperms than son-producing sperms. However it might in practice be done, imagine yourself as a parent trying to decide whether to have a son or a daughter. Again, we are not talking about conscious decisions but about the selection of generations of genes acting on bodies to influence the sex of their offspring.

If you were trying to maximize the number of your grandchildren, should you have a son or a daughter? We have already seen that you should have a child of whichever sex is in the minority in the population. That way, your child can expect a relatively large share of reproductive activity and you can expect a relatively large number of grandchildren. If neither sex is rarer than the other – if, in other words, the ratio is already 50:50 – you cannot benefit by preferring one sex or the other. It doesn't matter whether you have a son or a daughter. A 50:50 sex ratio is therefore referred to as evolutionarily stable, using the term coined by the great British evolutionist John Maynard Smith. Only if the existing sex ratio is something other than 50:50 does a bias in your choice pay. As for the question of why individuals should try to maximize their grandchildren and later descendants, it will hardly need asking. Genes that cause individuals to maximize their descendants are the genes we expect to see in the world. The animals we are looking at inherit the genes of successful ancestors.

It is tempting to express Fisher's theory by saying that 50:50 is the 'optimum' sex ratio, but this is strictly incorrect. The optimum sex to choose for a child is male if males are in a minority, female if females are in a minority. If neither sex is in a minority, there is no optimum: the well-designed parent is strictly indifferent about whether a son or a daughter will be born. Fifty-

fifty is said to be the evolutionary stable sex ratio because natural selection does not favor any tendency to deviate from it, and if there is any deviation from its natural selection favours a tendency to redress the balance.

Moreover, Fisher realized that it isn't strictly the numbers of males and females that are held at 50:50 by natural selection, but what he called the 'parental expenditure' on sons and daughters. Parental expenditure means all the hard-won food poured into the mouth of a child; and all the time and energy spent looking after it, which could have been spent doing something else, such as looking after another child. Suppose, for instance, that parents in a particular seal species typically spend twice as much time and energy on rearing a son as on rearing a daughter. Bull seals are so massive compared with cows that it is easy to believe (though probably inaccurate in fact) that this might be the case. Think what it would mean. The true choice open to the parent is not 'Should I have a son or a daughter?' but 'Should I have a son or *two* daughters?' This is because, with the food and other goods needed to rear one son, you could have reared two daughters. The evolutionary stable sex ratio, measured in numbers of bodies, would then be two females to every male. But *measured in amounts of parental expenditure* (as opposed to numbers of individuals), the evolutionarily stable sex ratio is still 50:50. Fisher's theory amounts to a balancing of the expenditures on the two sexes. This often, as it happens, turns out to be the same as balancing the numbers of the two sexes.

Even in seals, as I said, it looks as though the amount of parental expenditure on sons is not noticeably different from the amount spent on daughters. The massive inequality in weight seems to come about after the end of parental expenditure. So the decision facing a parent is still 'Should I have a son or a daughter?' Even though the total cost of a son's growth to adulthood may be much more than the total cost of a daughter's growth, if the additional cost is not borne by the decision maker (the parent) that's all that counts in Fisher's theory.

Fisher's rule about balancing the expenditure still holds in those cases where one sex suffers a higher rate of mortality than the other. Suppose, for instance, that male babies are more likely to die than female babies. If the sex ratio at conception is exactly 50:50, the males reaching adulthood will be outnumbered by the females. They are therefore the minority sex, and we'd naively expect natural selection to favor parents that specialize in sons. Fisher would expect this too, but only up to a point – and a precisely limited point, at that. He would not expect parents to conceive such a surplus of sons that the greater infant mortality is exactly compensated, leading to equality in the breeding population. No, the sex ratio at conception should be somewhat male-biased, but only up to the point where the total expenditure on sons is expected to equal the total expenditure on daughters.

Once again, the easiest way to think about it is to put yourself in the position of the decision-making parent and ask the question 'Should I have a daughter, who will probably survive, or a son, who may die in infancy?' The decision to make grandchildren via sons entails a probability that you'll have to spend more resources on some extra sons to replace those that are going to die. You can think of each surviving son as carrying the ghosts of his dead brothers on his back. He carries them on his back in the sense that the decision to go the son route to grandchildren lets the parent in for some additional wasted expenditure – expenditure that will be squandered on dead infant males. Fisher's fundamental rule still holds good. The total amount of goods and energy invested in sons (including feeding infant sons up to the point where they died) will equal the total amount invested in daughters.

What if, instead of higher male infant mortality, there is higher male mortality after the end of parental expenditure? In fact this will often be so, because adult males often fight and injure each other. This circumstance, too, will lead to a surplus of females in the breeding population. On the face of it, therefore, it would seem to favor parents who specialize in sons, thereby taking advantage of the rarity of males in the breeding population. Think a little harder, however, and you realize that the reasoning is fallacious. The decision facing a parent is the following: 'Should I have a son, who will likely be killed in battle after I've finished rearing him but who, if he survives, will give me extra specially many grandchildren? Or shall I have a daughter, who is fairly certain to give me an average number of grandchildren?' The number of grandchildren you can expect through a son is still the same as the average number you can expect through a daughter. And the cost of making a son is still the cost of feeding and protecting him up to the moment when he leaves the nest. The fact that he is likely to get killed soon after he leaves the nest does not change the calculation.

In all this reasoning, Fisher assumed that the 'decision maker' is the parent. The calculation changes if it is somebody else. Suppose, for instance, that an individual could influence its own sex. Once again, I don't mean influence by conscious intention. I am hypothesizing genes that switch an individual's development into the female or the male pathway, conditional upon cues from the environment. Following our usual convention, for brevity I shall use the language of deliberate choice by an individual – in this case, deliberate choice of its own sex. If harem-based animals like elephant seals were granted this power of flexible choice, the effect would be dramatic. Individuals would aspire to be harem-holding males, but if they failed at acquiring a harem they would much prefer to be females than bachelor males. The sex ratio in the population would become strongly female-biased. Elephant seals unfortunately can't reconsider the sex they were given at conception, but some fish can. Males of the blue-headed wrasse are large and bright-colored, and they hold harems of dull-colored females. Some females are larger than others, and they form a dominance hierarchy. If a male dies his place is quickly taken by the largest female, who soon turns into a bright-colored male. These fish get the best of both worlds. Instead of wasting their lives as bachelor males waiting for the death of a dominant, harem-holding male, they spend their waiting time as productive 27 females. The blue-headed wrasse sex-ratio system is a rare one, in which God's Utility Function coincides with something that a social economist might regard as prudent.

So, we've considered both the parent and the self as decision maker. Who else might the decision maker be? In the social insects the investment decisions are made, in large part, by sterile workers, who will normally be elder sisters (and also brothers, in the case of termites) of the young being reared. Among the more familiar social insects are honeybees. Beekeepers among my readers may already have recognized that the sex ratio in the hive doesn't seem, on the face of it, to conform to Fisher's expectations. The first thing to note is that workers should not be counted as females. They are technically females, but they don't reproduce, so the sex ratio being regulated according to Fisher's theory is the ratio of drones (males) to new queens being churned out by the hive. In the case of bees and ants, there are special technical reasons, which I have discussed in *The Selfish Gene* and won't rehearse here, for expecting the sex ratio to be 3:1 in favor of females. Far from this, as any beekeeper knows, the actual sex ratio is heavily male-biased. A flourishing hive may produce half a dozen new queens in a season but hundreds or even thousands of drones.

What is going on here? As so often in modern evolutionary theory, we owe the answer to W.D. Hamilton, now at Oxford University. It is revealing and epitomizes the whole Fisher-inspired theory of sex ratios. The key to the riddle of bee sex ratios lies in the remarkable phenomenon of swarming. A beehive is, in many ways, like a single individual. It grows to maturity, it reproduces, and eventually it dies. The reproductive product of a beehive is a swarm. At the height of summer, when a hive has been really prospering, it throws off a daughter colony – a swarm. Producing swarms is the equivalent of reproduction, for the hive. If the hive is a factory, swarms are the end product, carrying with them the precious genes of the colony. A swarm comprises one queen and several thousand workers. They all leave the parent hive in a body and gather as a dense cluster, hanging from a bough or a rock. This will be their temporary encampment while they prospect for a new permanent home. Within a few days, they find a cave or a hollow tree (or, more usually nowadays, they are captured by a beekeeper, perhaps the original one, and housed in a new hive).

It is the business of a prosperous hive to throw off daughter swarms. The first step in doing this is to make a 29 new queen. Usually half a dozen or so new queens are made, only one of whom is destined to live. The first one to hatch stings all the others to death. (Presumably the surplus queens are there only for insurance purposes.) Queens are genetically interchangeable with workers, but they are reared in special queen cells that hang below the comb, and they are fed on a specially rich, queen-nourishing diet. This diet includes royal jelly, the substance to which the novelist Dame Barbara Cartland romantically attributes her long life and queenly deportment. Worker bees are reared in smaller cells, the same cells that are later used to store honey. Drones are genetically different. They come from unfertilized eggs. Remarkably, it is up to the queen whether an egg turns into a drone or into a female (queen/worker). A queen bee mates only during a single mating flight, at the beginning of her adult life, and she stores the sperm for the rest of her life, inside her body. As each egg passes down her egg tube, she may or may not release a small package of sperm from her store, to fertilize it. The queen, therefore, is in control of the sex ratio among eggs. Subsequently, however, the workers seem to have all the power, because they control the food supply for the larvae. They could, for instance, starve male larvae if the queen laid too many (from their point of view) male eggs. In any case the workers have control over whether a female egg turns into a worker or a queen, since this depends solely on rearing conditions, especially diet.

Now let's return to our sex-ratio problem and look at the decision facing the workers. As we have seen, unlike the queen, they are not choosing whether to produce sons or daughters but whether to produce brothers (drones) or sisters (young queens). And now we are back to our riddle. For the actual sex ratio seems to be massively male-biased, which doesn't seem to make sense from Fisher's point of view. Let's look harder at the decision facing the workers. I said that it was a choice between brothers and sisters. But wait a moment. The decision to rear a brother is, indeed, just that: it commits the hive to whatever food and other resources it takes to rear one drone bee. But the decision to rear a new queen commits the hive to far more than just the resources needed to nourish one queen's body. The decision to rear a new queen is tantamount to a commitment to lay down a swarm. The true cost of a new queen only negligibly includes the small amount of royal jelly and other food that she will eat. It mostly consists of the cost of making all the thousands of workers who are going to be lost to the hive when the swarm departs.

This is almost certainly the true explanation for the apparently anomalous male bias in the sex ratio. It turns out to be an extreme example of what I was talking about earlier. Fisher's rule states that the quantity of expenditure on males and females must be equal, not the census count of male and female individuals. The expenditure on a new queen entails massive expenditure on workers who would not otherwise have been lost to the hive. It is like our hypothetical seal population, in which one sex costs twice as much as the other to rear, with the result that that sex is half as numerous. In the case of bees a queen costs hundreds or even thousands of times as much as a drone, because she carries on her back the cost of all the extra workers needed for the swarm. Therefore queens are hundreds of times less numerous than drones. There is an additional sting to this curious tale: when a swarm leaves, it mysteriously contains the *old* queen, not the new one. Nevertheless, the economics are the same. The decision to make a new queen still entails the outlay of the swarm needed to escort the old queen to her new home.

To round off our treatment of sex ratios, we return to the riddle of the harems with which we began: that profligate arrangement whereby a large herd of bachelor males consumes nearly half (or even more than half) the population's food resources but never reproduces nor does anything else useful. Obviously the economic welfare of the population is not being maximized here. What is going on? Once again, put yourself in the position of the decision maker – say, a mother trying to 'decide' whether to have a son or a daughter in order to maximize the number of her grandchildren. Her decision is, at naive first sight, an unequal one: 'Should I have a son, who will probably end up a bachelor and give me no grandchildren at all, or a daughter, who will probably end up in a harem and will give me a respectable number of grandchildren?' The proper reply to his would-be parent is 'But if you have a son, he *may* end up with a harem, in which case he'll give you far more grandchildren than you could ever hope to get via a daughter.' Suppose, for simplicity, that all the females reproduce at the average rate, and that nine out of ten males never reproduce, while one male in ten monopolizes the females. If you have a daughter, you can count on an average number of grandchildren. If you have a son, you have a 90 percent chance of no grandchildren but a 10 percent chance of having ten times the average number of grandchildren. The average number of grandchildren you can expect through your sons is the same as the average number you can expect through your daughters. Natural selection still favors a 50:50 sex ratio, even though species-level economic reason cries out for a surplus of females. Fisher's rule still holds.

I expressed all these reasonings in terms of 'decisions' of individual animals but, to repeat, this is just short-hand. What is really going on is that genes 'for' maximizing grandchildren become more numerous in the gene pool. The world becomes full of genes that have successfully come down the ages. How should a gene be successful in coming down the ages other than by influencing the decisions of individuals so as to maximize their numbers of descendants? Fisher's sex-ratio theory tells us how this maximizing should be done, and it is very different from maximizing the economic welfare of the species or population. There is a utility function here, but it is far from the utility function that would spring to our human economic minds.

The wastefulness of the harem economy can be summarized as follows: Males, instead of devoting themselves to useful work, squander their energy and strength in futile struggles against one another. This is true, even if we define 'useful' in an apparently Darwin-ian way, as concerned with rearing children. If males diverted into useful channels the energy that they waste competing with each other, the species as a whole would rear more children for less effort and less food consumed.

A work-study expert would stare aghast at the world of the elephant seal. An approximate parallel would be the following. A workshop needs no more than ten men to run it, since there are just ten lathes in the workshop. Instead of simply employing ten men, the management decides to employ a hundred men. Every day, all hundred men turn up and collect their wages. Then they spend the day fighting for possession of the ten lathes. Some items get made on the lathes, but no more than would have been achieved by ten men, and probably fewer, because the hundred men are so busy fighting that the lathes are not being used efficiently. The work-study expert would be in no doubt. Ninety percent of the men are redundant, and they should be officially declared so and dismissed.

It isn't just in physical combat that male animals waste their efforts – 'waste' being defined, once again, from the point of view of the human economist or work-study expert. In many species there's a beauty contest too. This brings us to another utility function that we humans can appreciate even though it doesn't make straightforward economic sense: aesthetic beauty. On the face of it, it might look as though God's Utility

Function is sometimes drawn up along the lines of the (now thankfully unfashionable) Miss World contest, but with males parading the runway. This is seen most clearly in the so-called leks of birds such as grouse and ruffs. A 'lek' is a patch of ground traditionally used by male birds for parading in front of females. Females visit the lek and watch the swaggering displays of a number of males before singling one out and copulating with him. The males of lekking species often have bizarre ornamentation, which they show off with equally remarkable bowing or bobbing movements and strange noises. The word 'bizarre' is, of course, a subjective value judgment; presumably lekking male sage grouse, with their puffed-up dances accompanied by cork-popping noises, don't seem bizarre to the females of their own species, and this is all that matters. In some cases the female birds' idea of beauty happens to coincide with ours, and the result is a peacock or a bird of paradise.

Nightingale songs, pheasant tails, firefly flashes and the rainbow scales of tropical reef fish are all maximizing aesthetic beauty, but it is not – or is only incidentally – beauty for human delectation. If we enjoy the spectacle it is a bonus, a by-product. Genes that make males attractive to females automatically find themselves passed down the digital river to the future. There is only one utility function that makes sense of these beauties; it is the same one that explains elephant-seal sex ratios, cheetahs and antelopes running superficially futile races against each other, cuckoos and lice, eyes and ears and windpipes, sterile worker ants and superfertile queens. The great universal Utility Function, the quantity that is being diligently maximized in every cranny of the living world is, in every case, the survival of the DNA responsible for the feature you are trying to explain.

Peacocks are burdened with finery so heavy and cumbersome that it would gravely hamper their efforts to do useful work, even if they felt inclined to do useful work – which, on the whole, they don't. Male songbirds use dangerous amounts of time and energy singing. This certainly imperils them, not only because it attracts predators but because it drains energy and uses time that could be spent replenishing that energy. A student of wren biology claimed that one of his wild males sang itself literally to death. Any utility function that had the long-term welfare of the species at heart, even the long-term survival of this particular individual male, would cut down on the amount of singing, the amount of displaying, the amount of fighting among males. Yet, because what is really being maximized is DNA survival, nothing can stop the spread of DNA that has no beneficial effect other than making males beautiful to females. Beauty is not an absolute virtue in itself. But inevitably, if some genes do confer on males whatever qualities the females of the species happen to find desirable, those genes, willy-nilly, will survive.

Why are forest trees so tall? Simply to overtop rival trees. A 'sensible' utility function would see to it that they were all short. They would get exactly the same amount of sunlight, with far less expenditure on thick trunks and massive supporting buttresses. But if they were all short, natural selection couldn't help favoring a variant individual that grew a little taller. The ante having been upped, others would have to follow suit. Nothing can stop the whole game escalating until all trees are ludicrously and wastefully tall. It is ludicrous and wasteful only from the point of view of a rational economic planner thinking in terms of maximizing efficiency. But it all makes sense once you understand the true utility function – genes are maximizing their own survival. Homely analogies abound. At a cocktail party, you shout yourself hoarse. The reason is that everybody else is shouting at top volume. If only the guests could come to an agreement to whisper, they'd hear one another exactly as well with less voice strain and less expenditure of energy. But agreements like that don't work unless they are policed. Somebody always spoils it by selfishly talking a bit louder, and, one by one, everybody has to follow suit. A stable equilibrium is reached only when everybody is shouting as loudly as physically possible, and this is much louder than required from a 'rational' point of view. Time and again, cooperative restraint is thwarted by its own internal instability. God's Utility Function seldom turns out to be the greatest good for the greatest number. God's Utility Function betrays its origins in an uncoordinated scramble for selfish gain.

Humans have a rather endearing tendency to assume that welfare means group welfare, that 'good' means the good of society, the future well-being of the species or even of the ecosystem. God's Utility Function, as derived from a contemplation of the nuts and bolts of natural selection, turns out to be sadly at odds with such utopian visions. To be sure, there are occasions when genes may maximize their selfish welfare at their level, by programming unselfish cooperation, or even self-sacrifice, by the organism at its level. But group welfare is always a fortuitous consequence, not a primary drive. This is the meaning of 'the selfish gene.'

Let us look at another aspect of God's Utility

Function, beginning with an analogy. The Darwinian psychologist Nicholas Humphrey made up an illuminating fact about Henry Ford. 'It is said' that Ford, the patron saint of manufacturing efficiency, once

> commissioned a survey of the car scrapyards of America to find out if there were parts of the Model T Ford which never failed. His inspectors came back with reports of almost every kind of breakdown: axles, brakes, pistons – all were liable to go wrong. But they drew attention to one notable exception, the *kingpins* of the scrapped cars invariably had years of life left in them. With ruthless logic Ford concluded that the kingpins on the Model T were too good for their job and ordered that in future they should be made to an inferior specification.

You may, like me, be a little vague about what kingpins are, but it doesn't matter. They are something that a motor car needs, and Ford's alleged ruthlessness was, indeed, entirely logical. The alternative would have been to improve all the other bits of the car to bring them up to the standard of the kingpins. But then it wouldn't have been a Model T he was manufacturing but a Rolls Royce, and that wasn't the object of the exercise. A Rolls Royce is a respectable car to manufacture and so is a

Model T, but for a different price. The trick is to make sure that either the whole car is built to Rolls Royce specifications or the whole car is built to Model T specifications. If you make a hybrid car, with some components of Model T quality and some components of Rolls Royce quality, you are getting the worst of both worlds, for the car will be thrown away when the weakest of its components wears out, and the money spent on high-quality components that never get time to wear out is simply wasted.

Ford's lesson applies even more strongly to living bodies than to cars, because the components of a car can, within limits, be replaced by spares. Monkeys and gibbons make their living in the treetops and there is always a risk of falling and breaking bones. Supposing we commissioned a survey of monkey corpses to count the frequency of breakage in each major bone of the body. Suppose it turned out that every bone breaks at some time or another, with one exception: the fibula (the bone that runs parallel to the shinbone) has never ever been observed to break in any monkey. Henry Ford's unhesitating prescription would be to redesign the fibula to an inferior specification, and this is exactly what natural selection would do too. Mutant individuals with an inferior fibula – mutant individuals whose growth rules call for diverting precious calcium away from the fibula – could use the material saved to thicken other bones in the body and so achieve the ideal of making every bone in the body equally likely to break. Or the mutant individuals could use the calcium saved to make more milk and so rear more young. Bone can safely be shaved off the fibula, at least up to the point where it becomes as likely to break as the next most durable bone. The alternative – the 'Rolls Royce' solution of bringing all the other components up to the standard of the fibula – is harder to achieve.

The calculation isn't quite as simple as this, because some bones are more important than others. I guess it is easier for a spider monkey to survive with a fractured heelbone than with a fractured armbone, so we should not literally expect natural selection to make all bones equally likely to break. But the main lesson we take away from the legend of Henry Ford is undoubtedly correct. It is possible for a component of an animal to be too good, and we should expect natural selection to favor a lessening of quality up to, but not beyond, a point of balance with the quality of the other components of the body. More precisely, natural selection will favour a leveling out of quality in both the downward and upward directions, until a proper balance is struck over all parts of the body.

It is especially easy to appreciate this balance when it is struck between two rather separate aspects of life: peacock survival versus beauty in the eyes of peahens, for instance. Darwinian theory tells us that all survival is just a means to the end of gene propagation, but this does not stop us partitioning the body into those components, like legs, that are primarily concerned with individual survival and those, like penises, that are concerned with reproduction. Or those, like antlers, that are devoted to competing with rival individuals versus those, like legs and penises, whose importance does not depend upon the existence of rival individuals. Many insects impose a rigid separation between radically different stages in their life history. Caterpillars are devoted to gathering food and growing. Butterflies are like the flowers they visit, devoted to reproducing. They do not grow, and they suck nectar only to burn it immediately as aviation fuel. When a butterfly reproduces successfully, it spreads the genes not just for being an efficient flying and mating butterfly but for being the efficient feeding caterpillar that it was, as well. Mayflies feed and grow as underwater nymphs for up to three years. They then emerge as flying adults that live only a matter of hours. Many of them are eaten by fish, but even if they were not they would soon die anyway, because they cannot feed and they do not even possess guts (Henry Ford would have loved them). Their job is to fly until they find a mate. Then, having passed on their genes – including the genes for being an efficient nymph capable of feeding underwater for three years – they die. A mayfly is like a tree that takes years to grow, then flowers for a single glorious day and dies. The adult mayfly is the flower that briefly blooms at the end of life and the beginning of new life.

A young salmon migrates down the stream of its birth and spends the bulk of its life feeding and growing in the sea. When it reaches maturity it again seeks out, probably by smell, the mouth of its native stream. In an epic and much-celebrated journey the salmon swims upstream, leaping falls and rapids, home to the head-waters from which it sprang a lifetime ago. There it spawns and the cycle renews. At this point there is typically a difference between Atlantic and Pacific salmon. The Atlantic salmon, having spawned, may return to the sea with some chance of repeating the cycle a second time. Pacific salmon die, spent, within days of spawning.

A typical Pacific salmon is like a mayfly but without the anatomically clear-cut separation between nymph and adult phases in the life history. The effort of swimming upstream is so great that it cannot pay to do it twice. Therefore natural selection favors individuals that put every ounce of their resources left into one 'big bang' reproductive effort. Any resources left after breeding would be wasted – the equivalent of Henry Ford's overdesigned kingpins. The Pacific salmon have evolved toward whittling down their postreproductive survival until it approaches zero, the resources saved being diverted into eggs or milt. The Atlantic salmon were drawn toward the other route. Perhaps because the rivers they have to mount tend to be shorter and spring from less formidable hills, individuals that keep some resources back for a second reproductive cycle can sometimes do well by it. The price these Atlantic salmon pay is that they cannot commit so much to their spawn. There is a trade-off between longevity and reproduction, and different kinds of salmon have opted for different equilibria. The special feature of the salmon life cycle is that the grueling odyssey of their migration imposes a discontinuity. There is no easy continuum between one breeding season and two. Commitment to a second breeding season drastically cuts into efficiency in the first. Pacific salmon have evolved toward an unequivocal commitment to the first breeding season, with the result that a typical individual unequivocally dies immediately after its single titanic spawning effort.

The same kind of trade-off marks every life, but it is usually less dramatic. Our own death is probably programmed in something like the same sense as that of the salmon but in a less downright and clear-cut fashion. Doubtless a eugenicist could breed a race of superlatively long-lived humans. You would choose for breeding those individuals who put most of their resources into their own bodies at the expense of their children: individuals, for example, whose bones are massively reinforced and hard to break but who have little calcium left over to make milk. It is easy enough to live a bit longer, if you are cosseted at the expense of the next generation. The eugenicist could do the cosseting and exploit the trade-offs in the desired direction of longevity. Nature will not cosset in this way, because genes for scrimping the next generation will not penetrate the future.

Nature's Utility Function never values longevity for its own sake but only for the sake of future reproduction. Any animal that, like us but unlike a Pacific salmon, breeds more than once faces trade-offs between the current child (or litter) and future children. A rabbit

that devoted all her energy and resources to her first

litter would probably have a superior first litter. But she would have no resources left to carry her on to a second litter. Genes for keeping something in reserve will tend to spread through the rabbit population, carried in the bodies of second- and third-litter babies. It is genes of this kind that so conspicuously did not spread through the population of Pacific salmon, because the practical discontinuity between one breeding season and two is so formidable.

As we grow older our chances of dying within the next year, after initially decreasing and then plateauing for a while, settle down to a long climb. What is happening in this long increase in mortality? It is basically the same principle as for the Pacific salmon, but spread out over an extended period instead of being concentrated in a brief precipitous orgy of death after the orgy of spawning. The principle of how senescence evolved was originally worked out by the Nobel laureate and medical scientist Sir Peter Medawar in the early 1950s, with various modifications to the basic ideas added by the distinguished Darwinians G. C. Williams and W. D. Hamilton.

The essential argument is as follows: first, as we saw in chapter 1, any genetic effect will normally be switched on at a particular time during the life of the organism.

Many genes are switched on in the early embryo, but others – like the gene for Huntington's chorea, the disease that tragically killed the folk poet and singer Woody Guthrie – are not switched on until middle age. Second, the details of a genetic effect, including the time at which it is switched on, may be modified by other genes. A man possessing the Huntington's chorea gene can expect to die from the disease, but whether it kills him when he is forty or when he is fifty-five (as Woody Guthrie was) may be influenced by other genes. It follows that by selection of 'modifier' genes the time of action of a particular gene can either be postponed or brought forward in evolutionary time.

A gene like the Huntington's chorea gene, which switches on between the ages of thirty-five and fifty-five, has plenty of opportunity to be passed on to the next generation before it kills its possessor. If, however, it were switched on at the age of twenty, it would be passed on only by people who reproduce rather young, and therefore it would be strongly selected against. If it were switched on at the age of ten, it would essentially never be passed on. Natural selection would favor any modifier genes that had the effect of postponing the age of switching on of the Huntington's chorea gene. According to the Medawar/Williams theory, this would be exactly why it normally does not switch on until middle age. Once upon a time it may well have been an early maturing gene, but natural selection has favored a postponing of its lethal effect until middle age. No doubt there is still slight selection pressure to push it on into old age, but this pressure is weak because so few victims die before reproducing and passing the gene on.

The Huntington's chorea gene is a particularly clear example of a lethal gene. There are lots of genes that are not in themselves lethal but nevertheless have effects that increase the probability of dying from some other cause and are called sublethal. Once again, their time of switching on may be influenced by modifier genes and therefore postponed or accelerated by natural selection. Medawar realized that the debilities of old age might represent an accumulation of lethal and sublethal genetic effects that had been pushed later and later in the life cycle and allowed to slip through the reproductive net into future generations simply because they were late-acting.

The twist that G. C. Williams, the doyen of modern American Darwinists, gave to the story in 1957 is an important one. It gets back to our point about economic trade-offs. To understand it, we need to throw in a couple of additional background facts. A gene usually has more than one effect, often on parts of the body that are superficially quite distinct. Not only is this 'pleiotropy' a fact, it is also very much to be expected, given that genes exert their effects on embryonic development and embryonic development is a complicated process. So, any new mutation is likely to have not just one effect but several. Though one of its effects may be beneficial, it is unlikely that more than one will be. This is simply because most mutational effects are bad. In addition to being a fact, this is to be expected in principle: if you start with a complicated working mechanism – like a radio, say – there are many more ways of making it worse than of making it better.

Whenever natural selection favors a gene because of its beneficial effect in youth – say, on sexual attractiveness in a young male – there is likely to be a downside: some particular disease in middle or old age, for example. Theoretically, the age effects could be the other way around but, following the Medawar logic, natural selection is hardly going to favor disease in the young because of a beneficial effect of the same gene in old age. Moreover, we can invoke the point about modifier genes again. Each of the several effects of a gene, its good and its bad effects, could have their switch-on times altered in subsequent evolution.

According to the Medawar principle, the good effects would tend to be moved earlier in life, while the bad effects would tend to be postponed until later. Moreover, there will in some cases be a direct trade-off between early and late effects. This was implied in our discussion of salmon. If an animal has a finite quantity of resources to spend on, say, becoming physically strong and able to leap out of danger, any predilection to spend those resources early will be favored over a preference to spend them late. Late spenders are more likely to be already dead from other causes before they have a chance to spend their resources. To put the general Medawar point in a sort of back-to-front version of the language we introduced in chapter 1, everybody is descended from an unbroken line of ancestors all of whom were at some time in their lives young but many of whom were never old. So we inherit whatever it takes to be young, but not necessarily whatever it takes to be old. We tend to inherit genes for dying a long time after we're born, but not for dying a short time after we're born.

To return to this chapter's pessimistic beginning, when the utility function – that which is being maximized – is DNA survival, this is not a recipe for happiness. So long as DNA is passed on, it does not matter who or what gets hurt in the process. It is better for the genes of Darwin's ichneumon wasp that the caterpillar should be alive, and therefore fresh, when it is eaten, no matter what the cost in suffering. Genes don't care about suffering, because they don't care about anything.

If Nature were kind, she would at least make the minor concession of anesthetizing caterpillars before they are eaten alive from within. But Nature is neither kind nor unkind. She is neither against suffering nor for it. Nature is not interested one way or the other in suffering, unless it affects the survival of DNA. It is easy to imagine a gene that, say, tranquilizes gazelles when they are about to suffer a killing bite. Would such a gene be favored by natural selection? Not unless the act of tranquilizing a gazelle improved that gene's chances of being propagated into future generations. It is hard to see why this should be so, and we may therefore guess that gazelles suffer horrible pain and fear when they are pursued to the death – as most of them eventually are. The total amount of suffering per year in the natural world is beyond all decent contemplation. During the minute it takes me to compose this sentence, thousands of animals are being eaten alive; others are running for their lives, whimpering with fear; others are being slowly devoured from within by rasping parasites; thousands of all kinds are dying of starvation, thirst and disease. It must be so. If there is ever a time of plenty, this very fact will automatically lead to an increase in population until the natural state of starvation and misery is restored.

Theologians worry away at the 'problem of evil' and a related 'problem of suffering.' On the day I originally wrote this paragraph, the British newspapers all carried a terrible story about a bus full of children from a Roman Catholic school that crashed for no obvious reason, with wholesale loss of life. Not for the first time, clerics were in paroxysms over the theological question that a writer on a London newspaper (*The Sunday Telegraph*) framed this way: 'How can you believe in a loving, all-powerful God who allows such a tragedy?' The article went on to quote one priest's reply: 'The simple answer is that we do not know why there should be a God who lets these awful things happen. But the horror of the crash, to a Christian, confirms the fact that we live in a world of real values: positive and negative. If the universe was just electrons, there would be no problem of evil or suffering.'

On the contrary, if the universe were just electrons and selfish genes, meaningless tragedies like the crashing 53 of this bus are exactly what we should expect, along with equally meaningless *good* fortune. Such a universe would be neither evil nor good in intention. It would manifest no intentions of any kind. In a universe of blind physical forces and genetic replication, some people are going to get hurt, other people are going to get lucky, and you won't find any rhyme or reason in it, nor any justice. The universe we observe has precisely the properties we should expect if there is, at bottom, no design, no purpose, no evil and no good, nothing but blind, pitiless indifference. As that unhappy poet A. E. Housman put it:

> For Nature, heartless, witless Nature
> Will neither care nor know.

DNA neither cares nor knows. DNA just is. And we dance to its music.

PHOENIX 60P PAPERBACKS

HISTORY/BIOGRAPY/TRAVEL
The Empire of Rome A.D. 98–190 *Edward Gibbon*
The Prince *Machiavelli*
The Alan Clark Diaries: Thatcher's Fall *Alan Clark*
Churchill: Embattled Hero *Andrew Roberts*
The French Revolution *E.J. Hobsbawm*
Voyage Around the Horn *Joshua Slocum*
The Great Fire of London *Samuel Pepys*
Utopia *Thomas More*
The Holocaust *Paul Johnson*
Tolstoy and History *Isaiah Berlin*

SCIENCE AND PHILOSOPHY
A Guide to Happiness *Epicurus*
Natural Selection *Charles Darwin*
Science, Mind & Cosmos *John Brockman, ed.*
Zarathustra *Friedrich Nietzsche*
God's Utility Function *Richard Dawkins*
Human Origins *Richard Leakey*
Sophie's World: The Greek Philosophers *Jostein Gaarder*
The Rights of Woman *Mary Wollstonecraft*
The Communist Manifesto *Karl Marx & Friedrich Engels*
Birds of Heaven *Ben Okri*

FICTION
Riot at Misri Mandi *Vikram Seth*
The Time Machine *H. G. Wells*

Love in the Night *F. Scott Fitzgerald*
The Murders in the Rue Morgue *Edgar Allan Poe*
The Necklace *Guy de Maupassant*
You Touched Me *D. H. Lawrence*
The Mabinogion *Anon*
Mowgli's Brothers *Rudyard Kipling*
Shancarrig *Maeve Binchy*
A Voyage to Lilliput *Jonathan Swift*

POETRY
Songs of Innocence and Experience *William Blake*
The Eve of Saint Agnes *John Keats*
High Waving Heather *The Brontes*
Sailing to Byzantium *W. B. Yeats*
I Sing the Body Electric *Walt Whitman*
The Ancient Mariner *Samuel Taylor Coleridge*
Intimations of Immortality *William Wordsworth*
Palgrave's Golden Treasury of Love Poems *Francis Palgrave*
Goblin Market *Christina Rossetti*
Fern Hill *Dylan Thomas*

LITERATURE OF PASSION
Don Juan *Lord Byron*
From Bed to Bed *Catullus*
Satyricon *Petronius*
Love Poems *John Donne*
Portrait of a Marriage *Nigel Nicolson*
The Ballad of Reading Gaol *Oscar Wilde*
Love Sonnets *William Shakespeare*
Fanny Hill *John Cleland*
The Sexual Labyrinth (for women) *Alina Reyes*
Close Encounters (for men) *Alina Reyes*